IMAGES OF
Peterborough

IMAGES OF
Peterborough

The Breedon Books
Publishing Company
Derby

First published in Great Britain by
The Breedon Books Publishing Company Limited
Breedon House, 44 Friar Gate, Derby, DE1 1DA.
1999

ISBN 1 85983 170 2

Printed and bound by Butler & Tanner Ltd., Selwood Printing
Works, Caxton Road, Frome, Somerset.

Colour separations and jacket printing by GreenShires Group
Ltd, Leicester.

Contents

Introduction

AS THE new century approaches, the time seems appropriate to look back, perhaps just a little dewy eyed, at how things were in Peterborough in days of yore – and some memories from not such distant times.

Peterborough has been many things to many people over the years and every era has left its mark on the city as we know it today – yes, even the Romans who settled here and developed a kingdom all of their own. Peterborough Museum has many amazing relics of their reign, and many more are being unearthed all the time.

Perhaps the only three constant factors in Peterborough over the centuries have been the magnificent Norman Cathedral, the River Nene, and the city's location which is as strategically blessed today, with its road and rail links, as it was to the Roman legions who recognised its potential as a base in their conquest to expand their empire across early Britain.

Roads, religion and the river, as you will see, figure prominently in this collection.

Much has been written about Peterborough in our newspapers – good news and bad news – and we have selected just a few of the pictures held in our archives which we hope will provide some nostalgic reflections of the city as we stand on the threshold of the year 2000.

We have tried to give as much information as possible to describe the pictures and the events they feature – although in the case of some of the older ones that go back 100 years or so, this has been difficult. But some of the photographs tell their own story and offer a fascinating glimpse of how life, fashions, transport, and the streets of the city were at the time the photographers captured them forever on film.

This book was never intended to be a history of Peterborough, it would take several volumes to accomplish that, rather it is a historical entertainment which we hope you enjoy.

Alex Gordon
Alan Cleaver

City Scenes

The first cut was the deepest. Estate agent and councillor Arthur Craig cutting the first sod for the foundations of the city's new Town Hall in the late 1920s.

Today it's Bridge Street and you can still recognise the Midland Bank building on the corner of Cathedral Square on the right, but in the 1920s it was called Narrow Street for obvious reasons. The buildings on the left were demolished to make way for new buildings, including the Town Hall.

Peterborough's original bridge over the River Nene. It was known locally as The Wooden Bridge, and was said to be 600 years old. This picture is *c.*1860.

The Golden Lion Commercial Hotel was popular with locals and travellers alike. It was located at the southern end of Narrow Street, where the Mothercare shop is today.

Construction of the current Town Bridge in 1931 to link the heart of the city's shopping area with Fletton and Woodston and to cope with increased traffic demand. In the background is Peterborough Power Station which is today the site of the Asda supermarket.

There were few traffic flow problems in Fletton Avenue when the driver of this lone horse and cart could take all the time in the world to make his journey. The picture is dated around 1910.

The builders were getting themselves into a right hole in this shot of construction on the new Town Bridge. The photographer was looking at work in progress from the junction of London Road and Oundle Road. The picture was taken around 1931 and The Iron Bridge that succeeded the old wooden one, can be seen on the left.

Fulbridge Road is a busy thoroughfare today but it was a scene of tranquillity in this leafy picture of Paston Valley in days gone by.

Westgate Mansion House pictured in August, 1911. The building was demolished in early 1920. Note the fine wrought-iron gates and the elegantly dressed ladies walking past.

Horses and cycles co-existed happily before World War One in the city's Gladstone Street. The cyclist's main problem was avoiding the horse droppings.

Exchange Street in 1901 showing part of the old almshouses in the forefront which in modern times became an Italian restaurant. Cathedral Square (out of shot) is on the right. Turning left would lead you into Queensgate and the Westgate Arcade.

Bridge Street as we know it today is almost recognisable from this 1920s shot taken from old warehouses which stood alongside the Iron Bridge which today marks the site of the Town Bridge. The area looked rather elegant with trees, shop awnings and pedestrians leisurely watching horse carriages and motor cars go by. The bridge was obviously a meeting place to stop for a chat.

Sunny days when cyclists and horse riders would stop for a drink at The Wheatsheaf in Alwalton village near Peterborough.

A rare shot of Werrington village before it became a popular area for city dwellers.

Cumbergate in the 1890s. Pub devotees will recognise the old – and much loved – Still at the far end of the picture. The road is now part of the Queensgate Centre at the entrance to Long Causeway. The tall building in the centre is the old GPO.

Busy Narrow Street, looking south in the 1920s and in the forefront is the Woodston bus – there was a notice on the wall on the right warning drivers to go slowly as the road narrowed down to just 15ft.

This farmer had come to town and was herding these sheep home that he had bought at the Cattle Market, along Westgate in the 1890s. Market Day was a real event in the city and people came from all over the area not only to buy farm livestock but domestic pets like rabbits too. The market with its hundreds of pens covered the whole of the current market area and the land occupied by Bayard Place.

It looks like a sister and brother pushing this pram along leafy Park Road when it was a much desired residential area in the early 1900s.

These gents with their shovels were perhaps working on the tram lines near the Post Office in Dogsthorpe when this picture was taken in 1901.

An atmospheric 1905 portrait of Peterborough Market Place – now Cathedral Square. You can see the Gates Memorial, a drinking fountain which was a tribute to Peterborough's first mayor, in the background. It was moved to the Bishop's Road gardens in the 1960s.

Long Causeway as it was around 1898. It was obviously taken in summer and all the shops had their awnings out to protect the goods in the windows. Note there was even a mini roundabout in those days, although this one had a gas lamppost in the middle.

A close up of Gates Memorial and a group of cyclists taking it easy in 1934.

Street scene of Westage in the 1920s.

Wide open spaces. The Guildhall dominates the picture and note the old gas lamppost on the right which was a meeting place for lots of 'gassing' when people took a seat for a chat.

Peterborough liked its ornate drinking fountains and this one was at The Triangle in New England. It looks like the ideal meeting place to stop for a few minutes on a sunny Sunday morning in 1912.

A very old picture of the Market Place (recognisable today as Cathedral Square) which was obviously taken in the early days of photography, around 1850 when long time exposures were necessary.

With the Queensgate shopping centre dominating the landscape today it is difficult to recognise Long Causeway as it was in the not-so-roaring twenties.

Lazy summer days were obviously quiet in the 1890s, even in the heart of the city's Market Place. The *Peterborough Advertiser*, once a sister paper of the *Evening Telegraph*, was started in the Printing Office you can see next to the Cathedral gateway.

Some people were so busy talking they didn't bother to get out of the way of the bicycles in Westgate in 1913.

Seen through the Cathedral gateway, work goes on turning Cathedral Square into a pedestrianised precinct in 1983.

A group of young girls face the camera in Lincoln Road East (now Burghley Road) in the early 1900s.

Everyone stopped for the camera in the early 1900s apparently. Locals pose for the photographer in Gladstone Street.

Long Causeway just after World War One, some soldiers can be seen in uniform. Note the tram line system in the middle of the road and in the distance a tram which was probably heading towards Walton.

One of the most popular places in Peterborough in 1923 was Hall's Auction Rooms in Exchange Street, where people could buy second-hand furniture at knock down prices. You had to descend some steps to enter the old shop.

Cars, trams, a horse cart and bicycles, all forms of transport co-existed in the city centre in the mid-1920s.

Gone to the dogs – two canines have St Paul's Road, New England, all to themselves in the kind of quiet street scene that just couldn't be taken today, c.early 1920s.

Soldiers on leave and civilians shop in Narrow Street during World War One. The shops in the forefront had both announced they were moving further along the street. Marks & Spencer's store would today be on the left.

Residential bliss. A shot of the corner of Huntly Grove and Granville Street.

In 1914 the building at the junction of City Road and New Road was the Peterborough Coffee House. It later served as the Ex-Servicemen's Club. The buildings were demolished to make way for Laxton Square and just beyond the new Passport Office is situated.

You would never guess from the sombre look of this picture that the event was the proclamation of the Bridge Fair in October 1929. The procession started from the Guildhall and wound it's way through town to the Fair Meadows in Oundle Road. Today's fair-goers don't take it quite so seriously.

Some scenes don't change quite as much as others. This was well-to-do Broadway, with the cemetery on the right, in the 1900s.

Looking from Oundle Road towards the Royal Oak in London Road in 1930. The properties were knocked down to make way for the new Town Bridge.

Narrow Street is coming down and the new Town Hall is going up in August, 1930 as modern Peterborough begins to take sl

HRH Prince George laying the foundation stone of the new Town Hall on June 28, 1929. Onlookers include Mayor Mr Arthur Craig and the Marquess of Exeter from Burghley House, Stamford, on the left.

Queen Street looking towards Westgate in 1973. The quiet little street was going to be transformed by the building of the multi-million pound Queensgate development.

Just another quiet day in Fitzwilliam Street in the heart of Peterborough. All Souls Church is on the right.

The Public Library is seen here being opened in Broadway by its donor, Mr Andrew Carnegie an American millionaire – from the Carnegie family of Carnegie Hall in New York fame. Mr Carnegie was pronounced the city's first Freeman at the same time, May, 1906.

Looking from Crescent Bridge in 1977 the scope of the Queensgate centre to come is obvious from the large area of vacant land that awaited its building.

The heart was being ripped out of the city – or so it seemed in 1978 when the major transformation that would be Queensgate got under way. The view of the Cathedral from this vantage point was soon to vanish.

The Nene Flows On

The River Nene has remained a constant factor in Peterborough, its course dictating development of the city. Over the years many people enjoyed walking by the river, and sailing on it, but in 1970, Walter Cornelius was the first person to try and fly across it. Walter landed in the drink, but that didn't stop him making another failed attempt later.

The big freeze of 1954 covered the River Nene in ice and snow. It produced this picturesque shot at Orton Staunch.

Messing about on the river by the Embankment at a regatta in 1948. The Cadge and Colman flour mill in East Station Road dominates the South Bank. Homeless people used to live in the moored houseboats but their vagrant way of life was sunk by a council order banning them in the 1960s.

An aerial shot from 1973 looking down the River Nene towards Town bridge. Brierley's supermarket is in the foreground on the left and then we can see Bridge Street police station. Beyond the bridge the Key Theatre is being built and a car park and the old bus station occupies the ground where the new court buildings stand. The Lido on the top left remains.

Looking across emerging Thorpe Wood golf course to the Nene River Bridge at Orton Longueville on the right and Longthorpe on the left. The old British Sugar factory in Oundle Road is clearly visible (top centre).

Before the Lido was opened in 1936, people swam in the River Nene and this was a safe spot called The Bathing Place at the bottom of River Lane.

Peterborough may have been a growing city in the 1970s but its country roots were never far away as this picture of Milton Ferry shows. It is now part of the Ferry Meadows country park development.

The city's two constant points of reference, the river and the Cathedral pictured in the early 1900s. The buildings include a boatyard and a timber merchant's.

An aerial view of the site of Peterborough's third bridge across the Nene which was to carry the new Frank Perkins Parkway, taken when work started in 1983.

Hammond's famous boats await people who want to go messing about on the river. The picture was taken in the 1920s and the chute which you can see clearly in the picture was used to channel snow cleared by horse and car, from city streets down into the river.

A more up to date aerial riverscape taken in 1989, showing the warehouse development on the South Bank.

Another shot of Hammond's boats and the Custom House – now the headquarters of the Sea Cadets – in the foreground.

A rare view of Orton Staunch in 1900 when the lock keeper's cottage stood on an island between the lock gates and the weir.

Looking down the river from Town Bridge towards the railway bridges in 1900. It makes a tranquil scene.

Fair Meadows in Oundle Road became part of the river during the great Peterborough Floods in August 1912. Town Bridge can be seen on the right. Some people obviously thought it was a good excuse for a summer paddle.

The new riverside walk along the Embankment in 1973 shortly after the bank was piled to stop it collapsing into the river. It provided city dwellers with a peaceful new amenity and better mooring facilities for people in boats too.

A jungle of metalwork goes up for the first new river bridge since the 1930s at Orton. It was to carry the new Nene Parkway. This picture was taken in the 1970s.

Winter's icy fingers made a spectacular view at the Embankment in January, 1983.

Another view of the Nene Parkway taking shape in 1974 and set to speed traffic through from Orton to Longthorpe.

The river has always played a vital role in Peterborough life and here it was again the focal point for a summer event. The picture was probably taken before World War One.

Don't rock the boat. A Peterborough Rowing Club event on the Nene in 1948.

The Bridge Fair arrives in Oundle Road in the 1890s with a colourful array of caravans.

City at War

Remembering the dead of World War One, civic dignitaries bow their heads on Armistice Sunday, 1922.

An Anzac is carried to his last resting place in Broadway cemetery in August 1916. Sgt Thomas Hunter was born in Newcastle, but emigrated to Kurrii Kurrii in New South Wales and fought in World War One with the Anzacs, the Australia and New Zealand Army Corps. He was wounded in the bloody battle of the Somme and evacuated to England. While on a train bound for Leeds his condition grew so bad that he was taken off at Peterborough station. He died shortly afterwards in Peterborough Hospital (now the Museum building). Local people paid for the 10ft high monument on his grave and a bronze commemorative plaque was placed on the wall of Peterborough Cathedral reading: 'In gratitude to the Lonely Anzac.'

Soldiers fire the last salute over the grave of Anzac Sgt Thomas Hunter.

Peterborough remembers a man that nobody knew in life – Sgt Thomas Hunter – but celebrated in death.

The 48th Northants Regiment visits Peterborough in 1913 as war clouds were gathering over Europe. These men would shortly see active service and many would not return.

They wanted to fight for their county. Men who had heeded the call to arms in the early days of World War One line up outside Peterborough's Recruiting Office.

The role of the nurses is marked in the Peace Proclamation celebrations of July 1919.

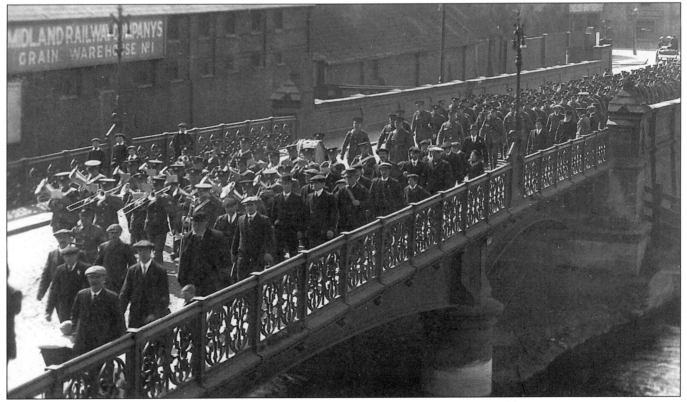

A march over the Iron Bridge by the men of the 2nd-5th Norfolk Regiment during World War One.

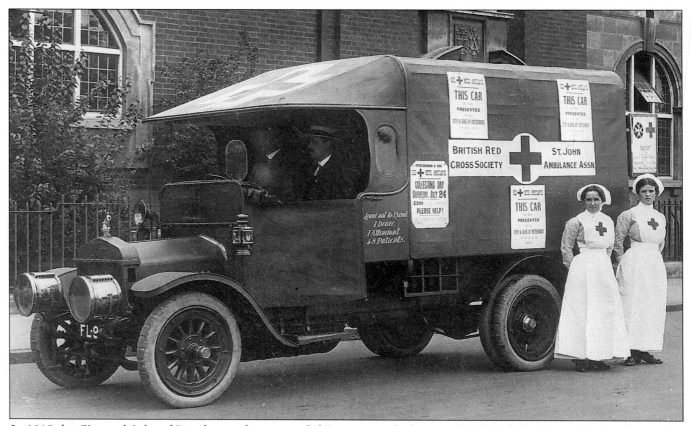

In 1915 the City and Soke of Peterborough presented this motor ambulance to the British Red Cross Society for service at the front. It was dedicated by the then Bishop of Peterborough, Dr Frank Theodore Woods. The ambulance cost £540 and £140 of that was from a generous benefactor who wished to remain anonymous. Driver was Mr Joseph Stephenson accompanied by Mr W. S. Abbott.

The Peace Celebration march of 1919 makes its way past cheering crowds in Broadway.

The local Fire Brigade take pride of place leading the Mayor in the Peace Celebration march in the Cathedral Precincts.

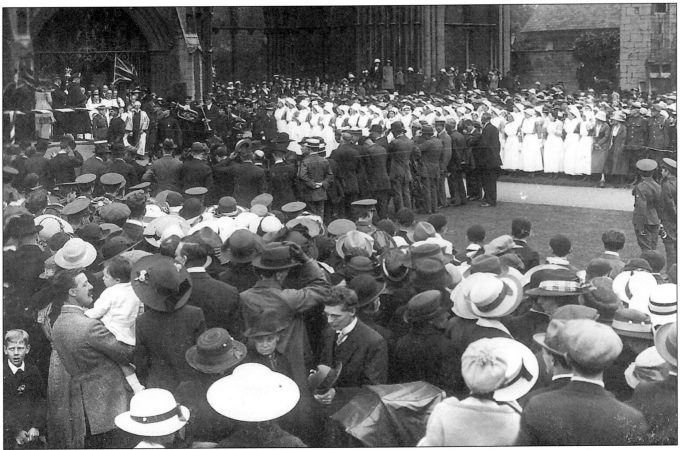

Praising the peace. This was the striking scene in front of the West Front of the Cathedral when crowds turned out to savour the glorious atmosphere.

The Belles from the Flax Factory at Woodston joined in the Peace Celebrations parade too.

Crying women folk accompany their men down Bridge Street to East Station as they set off for World War One.

Northants Battery parade in Peterborough in 1915.

These men will soon be swapping their straw boaters for tin helmets as they march off to World War One. They were due to board a train at the East Station.

A show of strength. With rifles over their shoulders, soldiers march down Bridge Street.

The Market Place is spilling over as the city gathers for the Peace Parade of 1919.

In the early stages of World War One the city was gripped by anti-German fever and the mayor was obliged to read the Riot Act on August 7, 1914, as crowds attacked a German butcher's shop in Westgate and a pub in Long Causeway. Windows were smashed, Westgate was littered with foodstuffs and hams were used as footballs. The troops had to be called in to restore order. A score of people were fined or bound over.

At the outbreak of World War One, in response to Lord Kitchener's 'Your country needs you', appeal 600 men who joined up made their way to the station en route to training camps.

The solemn occasion in July, 1919 when, in front of the Cathedral, the Deputy Mayor, Alderman I. Whitsted, read the proclamation declaring the end of World War One.

When World War Two broke out the city was ready once more. Here are the Head Wardens and deputies whose responsibility it was to alert the population to take cover and follow air-raid procedures.

Civil Defence organisers in their headquarters at the Town Hall in 1939.

The 1st Northants (City of Peterborough) Home Guard Battalion.

Peterborough Fire Service Week was marked in November 1942 by a stirring show at The Embassy, Peterborough.

Casualty of war. Number 37 Queen's Walk, New Fletton, after a German bombing raid on November 16, 1940. Mr and Mrs Crowson and their daughter Mary had a lucky escape.

VJ Day in 1945 was marked by a huge turn out at the Guildhall, which was still bricked up against any bomb damage.

Peterborough Home Guard City Battalion, No 3 Company, No 3 Platoon in 1940.

Somebody said that war consists of long periods of boredom and short bursts of excitement. This picture caught wardens waiting for something to happen.

Primitive looking equipment at the report centre at Peterborough Town Hall, but it was the vital link in the city's Civil Defence organisation.

It was enough to have grown men crying in their beer. This was the Coalheaver's Arms in Park Street on the morning after a raid on November 16, 1940. But the pub opened for business that night as usual.

Peterborough Mayor Harry Farrow making two American Air Force sergeants welcome outside the Town Hall in 1943.

— 59 —

Private cars were adapted for Civil Defence work. This one was pictured hauling an auxiliary fire pump for the Walton fire crew in Sages Lane.

A crashed Junkers JU 88 photographed at the King's School during a tour of the country in War Weapons Week 1940.

Damage to Peterborough Swimming Pool (now the Lido) during the first air raid on the city on June 8, 1940.

The scene in London Road after a raid on November 16, 1940. One woman received a bruised leg but all occupants were safely rescued out of a bedroom window.

Americans leading a the VE Day parade to the Cathedral in 1945.

Collecting aluminium pots and pans outside the Guildhall in 1940 for the war effort.

Stirring scenes outside the Cathedral at the 1945 VE Day parade.

Peterborough air raid wardens ran a recruiting campaign at the Odeon cinema in August, 1939.

The first Nazi bomber seen in the city, the captured Junkers, being paraded through the city. The policeman is the late Ron Forth.

A WVS mobile canteen attracts hungry soldiers in the Market Place.

Celebrating in Highbury Street, Peterborough with a VE Day party on May 8, 1945.

Special Constables line up outside the Sessions House in Thorpe Road in the early days of World War Two.

Baker Perkins staff carrying out gas mask drill in the early days of the war.

On the Move

Trams were a familiar sight on the streets of Peterborough from the turn of the century until 1930. Here a local crew of driver and conductor posed for the camera.

Look out dear here comes the future. A tram catches up with a couple in their horse-drawn buggy in Westgate before World War One.

A tram waits at the Terminus in the Market Place for passengers.

Staff and officials proudly line up at Millfield tram depot with the Walton service tram. The lack of advertising round the upper deck of the vehicle would suggest that it is just entering service in 1903.

Again the tram is seen as a new fangled modern invention existing alongside the trusty horse and carriage in this shot of Midgate. But people at the time hated the noise of the vehicles as Peterborough had been a tranquil place until their clattering arrival.

Another era in travel was marked when this fragile looking flying machine became the first aircraft to land in Peterborough in June, 1912. At the controls was Mr W. H. Ewen, who was known as The Daily Mail Airman because of his sponsorship by the national newspaper for his flying exploits. He was presented with a memento of his landing by the Mayor. But disaster struck when he crashed on take off and the plane was damaged. It took Mr Ewen's engineer some time to fix it.

A panoramic shot of Long Causeway and another meeting of two eras, the carriage and the tram, at the turn of the century.

Local shops soon wakened up to the potential of advertising on the trams, here Barretts and Rogers are proudly displayed on vehicles bound for Newark and Walton. Their advertising was obviously on the right lines.

The horse drawn Horrell's Dairy milk floats became a familiar sight in the city as people enjoyed their pinta on the doorstep service. Here the milkmen were pictured at the Westwood Farm dairy in 1954.

An early picture of Donald's garage in Burghley Road, which is still there today. At the time they were dealers for the popular Austin cars.

Whatever the occasion the trams were packed leaving Long Causeway and all the ladies were done up in their finery in this picture from the early 1900s. Perhaps they were going to Peterborough Show.

Bikes and trikes, the trams would never replace them. This is an advertising shot of J. Pacey's cycle shop in Lincoln Road.

Well-known city cycle enthusiast the late Cyril Munday pictured with one of his wonderful old bikes in 1972.

No wonder Albert Scrimshire looks proud as punch in this 1929 picture, he's in charge of what's thought to have been Britain's first diesel lorry. Mr Scrimshire worked for the then Barford and Perkins in Queen Street – the forerunners of the mighty Perkins diesel engine giant. He drove a six-wheel tipper truck mounted on a Sentinels chassis and powered by a Gardner diesel engine with a Mercedes-Benz supercharger. It is thought that Frank Perkins was so impressed by the truck he decided to build a diesel engine of his own. The rest as they say, is history.

The age of the bus was booming when this picture of Peterborough Bus Station was taken in the late 1930s. Trams were already history.

Garages have nearly all moved to the outskirts of Peterborough today, but in February,1950, Reed's was situated in Broadway. If the building looks familiar it is because it was bought by the *Peterborough Advertiser* company and became the headquarters of the newspaper.

Another commercial picture which was used to extol the virtues of buying a cycle from Pell & Parker's Cycle Factors & Makers shop on the corner of Westgate and Cromwell Road.

Traction engines chug along Lincoln Road billowing steam at Boroughbury corner with Westgate in the late 1890s. Note the delivery boy with his distinctive basket walking across the forefront of the picture.

If you wanted a Hillman car in the 1930s this garage in Westgate was the place to visit. A shiny new model is seen taking to the road.

Modern times. Bridge Street in August, 1955, when buses and their parking spaces were given number one priority. High Street names like Halford's, Dolcis, James Walker the Jewellers, and Burton's were much in evidence. Pedestrianisation had not even been thought of back then.

At the junction of Westgate and Queen Street before World War One, Heighton's specialised in Vinco cycles, powered tricycle-carriages and Darracq cars.

It was someone's New Year greeting for 1929 but it found its way into the *Evening Telegraph* library. We believe it's a shot of a taxi cab waiting outside Peterborough North Station. Both men look as if they may have been drivers.

This picture of an old filling station in Newark, Peterborough, obviously wasn't taken at rush hour. A petrol station surrounded by trees is certainly a quaint sight.

The city's first traffic warden Mr Fred Peck casts a suspicious eye over a Mark I Ford Cortina in New Road in May 1966.

Cars, bikes, motorcycles and a sign that proclaimed 'Cars For Hire' at Laxton's garage in Lincoln Road.

A schoolboy gets the chance of rare close up view of Nazi chief Goering's staff car when it was sent for restoration at a specialist's in Baston, near Peterborough, in 1972.

Once they had housed the railwaymen of Peterborough but the days were already numbered for many of the Great Northern Cottages in New England – known locally as 'The Barracks' – in 1969 because they lacked many mod-cons.

Your carriage awaits you. There was a line-up of carriages for travellers getting off trains at the Peterborough East railway station in 1910. On the left is a Great Eastern Railway horse-powered delivery truck.

The still-familiar frontage of Peterborough North Station taken around 1910.

The Great Eastern level crossing, gateway to the city from London Road in the early 1930s.

Peterborough North Railway station undergoes modernisation work in November, 1976.

Crunch! A train derailment. The locomotive lies on its side, its tender crumpled behind it on the line near Westwood Bridge, outside Baker Perkins factory in September, 1955. Luckily the train was travelling slowly when it left the rails and only five people were slightly injured.

In August, 1913, some 40 foundrymen at the Great Northern Railway engineering works in Westwood Street came out on strike following the dismissal of a moulder for throwing a blank cartridge into a hot ladle. They refused to return until he was reinstated and they claimed it was 'tyranny' by the man's foreman. The 'blacklegs' who continued to work were escorted to and from work by jeering strikers carrying placards proclaiming their business. There was talk of a national strike but the NUR refused to back it and the protest petered out.

Two smartly-dressed students from the Peterscourt Training College stride out of the city's Thorpe Road subway underneath the railway line. The subway replaced a pedestrian route through the level crossings after a woman was killed by a train. The subway was itself replaced by Crescent Bridge.

Crescent Bridge under construction in 1912. The North Station is in the background behind the level crossing gates, with the subway building on the right.

A view of St Leonard's Street *c.*1930. The picture is taken from the direction of the Six Bells pub. Notice the adverts on the left for the latest films *Professional Soldier, Music Is Magic* and a Max Miller comedy showing at the Palace in Broadway and the City in Bridge Street.

A fine view of the North Station and the great Northern Hotel taken around 1910.

The days of traffic congestion in the city centre were numbered as work on pedestrianisation began in Long Causeway in 1983. Trees were about to make a comeback too.

The opening of the new Crescent Bridge on April 16, 1913. The civic dignitaries look imposing in their top hats.

An aerial view of the Eye bypass being built on the route of the old M&GN Railway, looking towards Peterborough, in 1991.

Sainsbury's store at Bretton being built in advance of many of the township's houses in the early 1970s. The changes wrought on the landscape by the building of the superb parkway road system is obvious. The fields at the top (centre) of the picture became the site of Edith Cavell hospital.

Bridge that gap. The city's third bridge over the Nene and the railway line was built to carry the parkway traffic.

Lincoln Road pictured as the city's parkway system was constructed in the 1970s. Work was underway to create the present busy roundabout. To the left of the main road is the old Peter Brotherhood factory. Work began on Greater Peterborough's first urban motorway – from Lincoln Road to the A47 near Milton Ferry – in October 1970. The first stage of the Western Primary Road, as it was called, cost £2 million.

It was full steam ahead on the Nene Valley Railway in 1984. It has proved both a boon to steam fans and tourists from all over the country. Not to mention movie makers who have used the railway for many films, including two James Bond action-adventure features.

A beautiful shot of Westgate in the 1920s. The Elephant & Castle and the Royal Hotel are on the right.

Emergencies

A long-ago memory survives in this faded picture of men preparing one of Peterborough's first steamer fire engines.

Peterborough Volunteer Firemen ready for action in 1904 with their hand-drawn hose cart. One man proudly holds a trophy won in a fire brigade competition. The helmets were magnificent.

A dramatic floodlit scene when firemen fought a blaze at Westgate Congregational Church in 1983.

A Peterborough Borough Police line-up in 1890. The picture was taken at their headquarters in Milton Street.

Well ablaze. A fire at English Brothers' timber yard on the South Bank in the early 1960s.

The City Police proudly strike up a pose in 1908.

The Black Bridge at Stanground blazes from end to end in 1963. The rail bridge was covered in pitch and tar to preserve it, but it turned out to be its undoing because it fuelled the flames.

The Westwood Works (Baker Perkins) was gutted in the great fire of 1922, as shown above and next page.

The scene of destruction in King Street in August, 1956 after the Robert Sayle's store caught fire and flames spread across the street to ignite the firm's other building on the right.

The burned out shell of Queen Street Baptist Chapel after an inferno in 1905.

The remnants of Frank Brierley's famous cut price store in Bridge Street after a blaze which gutted the premises in May 1968.

A dynamic shot of the city's biggest ever fire when the Robert Sayle store in Cowgate was destroyed in a blaze that caused damage amounting to a quarter of a million pounds.

A very early version of the fire brigade's extension ladder was used in this incident in Park Road.

The river ran through the streets of Stanground when the lode overflowed in August 1912. The Co-op staff and customers watched anxiously as the water level rose.

Floods at Stanground when the lode rose 8ft above normal flooding the street up to a depth of 4ft. This 1912 picture shows the Fletton High Street end. The man in the forefront was carrying the photographer on a punt.

People took refuge up ladders and laid planks to get from house to house when when the river rose and flooded the area known as Bodger's Yard in 1912.

The 1912 flood caused Oundle Road to be almost impassable under the railway bridge – and it still floods there to this day.

The river runs through it (normally) but it almost ran over the Town Bridge – to the astonishment of onlookers – in 1912.

Today it's the Asda supermarket car park, but in 1912 it was School Place and the residents were left high and dry by the flood waters.

The Crowland floods of 1947 when the banks burst and water roared through the breach in the dyke.

The flooded scene in Crowland Road looking towards Mason's Bridge. The breach in the north level barrier flooded 20,000 acres of agricultural land to a depth of several feet.

The occupants of Steam House Farm (left) must have felt that they had moved to the seaside when the Crowland floods lapped at their doorstep in 1947.

A flash flood in Midgate being pumped out in 1924 when the drains could not cope with the surge of water.

The Perkins Diesel Fire Brigade lined up for this picture at the Queen Street works.

The London Brick Fire Brigade on parade with their equipment. Companies were expected to look after own fire safety in years gone by.

On March 22, 1989 the city was rocked by a massive explosion in the Fengate industrial area. A lorry packed with explosives blew up outside the factory of a plant hire firm. A fireman was killed and dozens of people were seriously injured in the explosion which demolished the Vibroplant factory and sent debris flying hundreds of yards. The huge blast was heard over 10 miles away as it ripped through Fengate wrecking nearby factories and tearing out windows up to a quarter of a mile away. The lorry had been on its way to deliver its cargo to a fireworks factory when the blast happened. It left a crater 10ft wide and 2ft deep. Eye-witnesses described the scene as one of 'absolute devastation' and said cars had 'melted beyond recognition'. The real miracle was that more people were not killed.

Making a Living

One of the city's most celebrated sons, diesel engine giant Frank Perkins receiving the Freedom of the City from Mayor, Charles Swift in 1962.

When Perkins produced the 100,000th P6 diesel engine from the Eastfield factory in 1952, the engine was presented by Mr Frank Perkins to the University of Toronto.

The brick industry locally was biting the dust as some of the giant brickyard chimneys were blown up in March 1978.

Hereward Centre was considered to be the most modern of its kind in the pre-Queensgate era. This picture was taken in 1976.

Peter Brotherhood Ltd in Lincoln Road in 1992. This is now the site of the Safeway supermarket. Brotherhoods fame was already established when the engineering company came to Peterborough from Compton Street in London in 1907.

Midgate House in 1976. It stands on the old Barrett's Corner site, another local name that has long since passed into history.

Baker Perkins foundry workers line up for the camera.

A shot of Midgate when Barrett's store was boarded up – it was a symbol of the past across the road from the new Hereward Centre. The picture comes from 1972.

Peter Brotherhood Ltd played a big part in establishing the city's industrial base of heavy engineering. This shot inside the factory was taken in 1974.

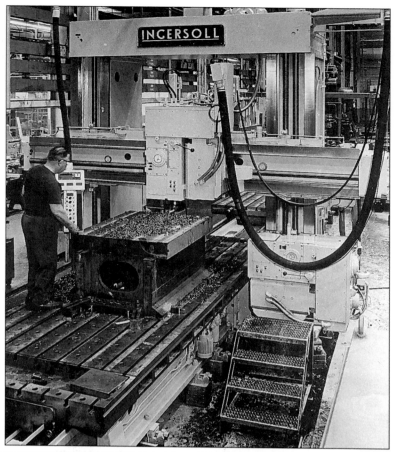

An aerial shot of Symington's corset factory in Bread Street, Fletton.

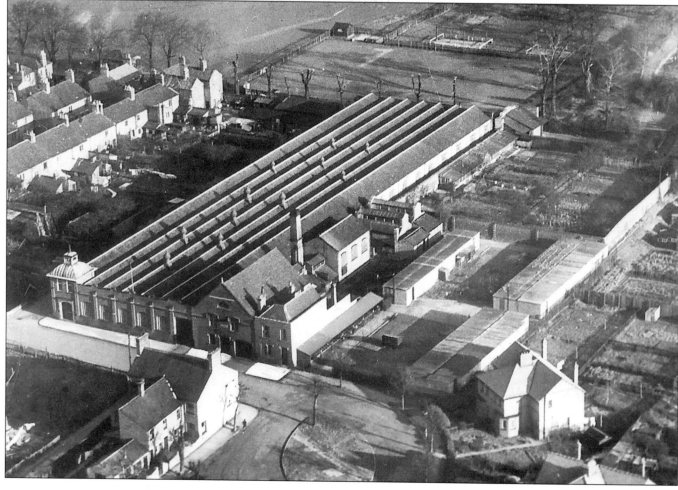

This picture of Hicks Brick Pit shows men digging clay benches. It is very rare and was probably taken before World War One. The area is now part of the Southern Township development.

Inside the factory of one of the other engineering greats who helped to bring employment to the city. This was Newall Engineering in High Street, Fletton, in 1977. Newall's was renowned for its precision engineering and one high profile contract was to make cameras for the Rank Organisation after the war and Newall's also worked on a prototype for a new Technicolor camera for the cinema.

Another city landmark – the Cadge & Colman flour mill in East Station Road on the South Bank of the river.

Another landmark – only recently demolished to make way for a new housing project – the British Sugar factory in Oundle Road. This is a 1989 picture.

A civic gathering in June, 1929, to celebrate the extension to Peterborough power station.

A shale-planer digging knots at Whittlesey brick-pits, leaving the characteristic neat and even face.

Brotherhood produced a large number of tractors during the 1920s many of which were exported, principally to Australia and New Zealand. The picture shows the power take off being used for thrashing corn.

The British Sugar factory was working flat out in the early-1970s and the annual beet season produced the infamous pong from the processing, and it was a constant source of complaint as it could be smelt from miles around. Tractors hauling beet from farms in the Fens to the factory in Oundle Road also created traffic congestion.

Another industry of bygone days – stonemasons at G. R. Dickens and Son in Eastfield Road in the early part of the century. Part of their craft was making gravestones to the individual requirements of the bereaved.

This picture will bring back memories for old Peterborians. In the foreground is the original St Mary's Church in New Road. Dominating the picture is the old gas works – all that remains today is the giant gasometer. Much of the gas works site is now occupied by the Boongate roundabout and the road to the Frank Perkins Parkway.

Charles Chapman, co-founder with Frank Perkins of F. Perkins Ltd (later to be the famous Perkins Engines Ltd) on his last visit to Peterborough in 1978 with the first Perkins six cylinder engine, the P6 which he designed in 1936.

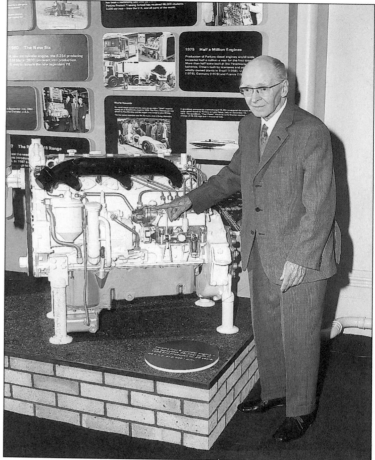

Beginning of the end of the Fletton brickyards in 1970. The brick pits have been filled in with power station fly ash which the men are damping down to stop it blowing away. It was then covered with soil and allowed to settle. It is now all part of the Southern Township re-development.

Skilled engineers at work in Baker Perkins engineering factory. The firm was an amalgamation of a number of engineering firms principally in 1919 of Perkins Engineers Ltd and Joseph Baker & Sons Ltd. But in 1923 the name became abbreviated to Baker Perkins. The firm became famous for making heavy machinery from biscuit machinery and ovens to printing presses.

Workers at the brick pits in Whittlesey around the mid-1920s. It was a dirty and dusty job, but men were glad to do it to earn a living for their families. Many of Peterborough's Italian immigrants took jobs in the brickyards after the war.

A sunny day in Broadway in 1978 and shoppers peruse the plants outside Peach's the florist. Across the road was the Fairways store which amongst other things sold toys. The row of shops on the right was demolished to make way for the new Central Library.

An interesting example of a Brotherhood three cylinder Radial Engine coupled to a dynamo. This picture, taken in France in 1880, shows an auto locomobile as it was styled, with Mr Peter Brotherhood at the controls.

The Boroughbury end of Lincoln Road and there's only one car in sight as shoppers linger in this 1972 picture.

The idea of the working woman isn't so new. These are the girls operating the sewing machines at Symington's corset factory in New Fletton. The factory was build in 1903 and the firm was the largest employer of female labour in the area.

Business was booming for the cycle shops in the 1920s. This is Bob Woodman & Cos at the corner of Bread Street and Oundle Road.

Open all hours. One of Home & Colonial's traditional grocery shops in Narrow Street in 1926. the supermarket generation will find the idea of the staff actually serving you rather novel. Note the price of margarine, 10 old pence and a packet of tea was 5 old pence a quarter.

Tinned food has been popular for a long time and here is the scene inside Farrow's canning factory in Fletton Avenue. The factory was opened in 1914 and in 1931 the firm installed a plant for canning peas and fruit to export round the world and in all corners of the globe tins could be seen bearing the legend Farrow's of Peterborough. Again the factory provided employment for women who wanted, or needed, to work to support their families.

Mario Pignatiello (centre) and his father Pasquale (on the left) came from Italy to Peterborough after the war. They were tempted to emigrate by London Brick and promises of jobs. Mario went on to become a successful businessman and a leader of an Italian community of around 5,000.

It was one of the best known and popular stores in its day, but Shelton's and its next door neighbour, the Odeon cinema, both closed as times changed down Broadway. Many of the shops on the right started out as private residencies until commerce spread outwards from the city centre.

The *Citizen & Advertiser* offices in Broadway in the mid-1960s before the newspaper headquarters moved to Woodston.

Goodness knows what the health inspectors would make of this. But back in the early 1900s Mutton Day was a popular event at the Nag's Head at Eastrea near Whittlesey. A storers charity bought a flock of sheep at Peterborough market and gave the meat away to 120 people at local pubs.

Another Broadway scene from 1950.

Many people will remember the days of coffee bars and quick snacks, like hot dogs and a large size grill for 4/6d at the Granville Cafe in Bridge Street in the 1960s. It made way for extensions to Brierley's store on the corner.

Lighting up peoples lives in the 1950s was Peterborough General Electric Co Ltd in Cowgate.

Another classic Peterborough name was Trollope's a leading clothes shop on the corner of Westgate and Queen Street. This picture was taken in June 1969.

Some traditional family businesses have survived, through all the changes in Peterborough, for decades. Like Frank Bros the pork butchers. The firm is 123 years old. This picture was of their old shop in Bridge Street before they moved to Park Road.

The Marks & Spencer store in Bridge Street in 1932. It was on the corner of Wentworth Street. The current store was opened just a few yards away in 1964 on the site of the old City Cinema.

This will bring back misty memories for smokers – the old Will Blackman tobacco stores in Long Causeway. And while you were buying your cigarettes or favourite pipe tobacco you could book for a trip to Skegness at the same time.

Cumbergate in 1928 with the old GPO building in the forefront and The Cosy Tea Rooms next door. The building on the extreme right was the old Trustee Savings Bank.

The old Freeman Hardy Willis shoe shop in Bridge Street was being refitted in 1965 when workmen came across this amazing discovery – the old beams were advertising a long-vanished Penny Bazaar shop called The Little Wonder.

Leisure & Pleasure

The old Six Bells Inn in Westgate in 1924. Peterborough was renowned for its traditional old street pubs.

Quiet tree-lined Dogsthorpe Village with The Bluebell pub. It is *c*.1930s and the tram lines can still be seen. The pub is still a popular local today.

In keeping with its pub town image of old, Peterborough Beer Festival has put the city on the discerning drinkers map. This is a scene from the 1990 event in a marquee at the Embankment.

The Black Horse Inn near the corner of Westgate and Lincoln Road in 1900.

The terminus for horse-drawn buses was conveniently next to the old Fox and Hounds pub at Longthorpe around 1908. The pub burned down in 1922 and the new trams drove the horse-drawn buses out of the city centre. For them it was the beginning of the end.

Bishops Road corner with Bridge Street, and the City Commercial Hotel was a popular hostelry and stopping place for travellers in the 1930s.

Travellers using the Great North Road had for decades found the Norman Cross Hotel a welcome oasis. This picture was taken in the 1950s.

This could be the landlord and a customer taking his ale away in a can, posing outside The Golden Lion in Oundle Road, Woodston.

The late Roy Kinnear came roaming round Peterborough as he had appeared as a Roman centurion on a TV commercial for Peterborough Development Corporation selling the benefits of moving to the new city. The late Roy, who was already well known for his TV and film work, boasted about the benefits of The Peterborough Effect.

Anybody who finds Oundle Road a bit of a headache with traffic these days will be amazed to realise that this is the same road in 1890. But the Gordon Arms is still very recognisable.

You lucky people – fans got a chance to see comedian Tommy Trinder open the new Broadway bingo hall in November, 1963.

This was soon to become the site of Peterborough's popular leisure amenity at Ferry Meadows. But it looked like a huge building site in 1978. The rubble was used as hardcore for the new city parkway road system and the hole left behind was flooded to create the artificial lakes which are so popular today.

Comedy legend Ernie Wise lived in Peterborough for a time and he and partner Eric Morecambe filmed scenes for one of their popular TV Christmas specials at Sibson airfield in November, 1972.

Henry the Train, a firm favourite with children visiting Ferry Meadows – and some of them arrive on a full-size steam train on the Nene Valley Railway.

An early aerial shot by the *Peterborough Advertiser* of Peterborough Show Grounds, *c*.1920.

Sailing on Ferry Meadows in 1979.

The crowds enjoying the delights of Peterborough Show, when it was situated at Eastfield, in 1950.

Families enjoy a day by the lake at Ferrymeadows in 1987. It was certainly closer than going to Sunny Hunny.

Shire horses parade in the Main Ring before the visitors to Peterborough Show at Eastfield in 1950.

Leisurely days in Central Park and the old bandstand. It was devoured by woodworm and had to be pulled down. It was replaced by a willow tree, but now there are plans to build a new bandstand and restore the park to its Victorian splendour.

A general view of the Peterborough Agricultural Society's 150th anniversary show in 1947 when the Showground was situated in Eastfield.

It was skiffle and all that jazz when The Thunderbolts band took the stage in 1952.

Many local people will remember with affection the old City Cinema and cafe in Bridge Street. The building, for many years a prominent feature of the city centre, cost £20,000 when it was opened on March 31, 1927. The cinema employed an orchestra to accompany films and a year or so after opening the City Cinema showed its first talkie, The Singing Fool with Al Jolson. The building was demolished to make way for Marks & Spencer, which opened its new store on the site in 1964.

Swing was the thing at The Grand in 1954 when dancers loved the sound of the big bands.

The Broadway Kinema pictured in the early days of World War Two was always crowded for the Saturday morning matinee. Many of the children in the picture were evacuees. The Kinema was packed at night too as families enjoyed a film but had to be prepared for air-raid warnings. The film showing on this occasion was Against The Wind starring Jack Warner, who was later to become famous on television as Dixon of Dock Green.

The Carolas Dance Band in full swing at the old Angel Hotel. The band was led by Tommy Joyce (on the left playing saxophone), and Tommy was also choirmaster at the London Road Methodist Chapel for 36 years and bandmaster in the Belvedere Orchestra.

The finishing touches being put to The Hippodrome variety theatre in Broadway in 1907, ready for its big opening night. It was built for entrepreneur Fred Karno (of Fred Karno's Army fame) who introduced variety acts to the city's entertainment scene. There was one drawback though, The Hippodrome had a tin roof and on more than one occasion the show was brought to a halt because of the noise during heavy rain.

The Third Anniversary line-up of the Court Players Company in 1941. They became a resident attraction at the old Theatre Royal and Empire Theatre after arriving in 1938 for for what should have been a six week run. Twenty years later, to celebrate their record of 1,000 successive performances, the Duke and Duchess of Gloucester went to see their show.

Peterborough's centre of entertainment in Broadway around 1913 with the Broadway Kinema on the left and The Hippodrome on the right. In the centre of the frame is The Empire Theatre.

Panto rehearsal at The Embassy in 1961.

The Grand Theatre, which was renamed The Empire. The picture is dated 1919.

The popular George Fovargue Band at the Grand Hotel in 1939.

The Bridge Fair tradition lives on – although it looks a lot brighter in 1991 than in our pictures of the early days.

Another popular Peterborough attraction in the 1940s, Dennis Martell and His Orchestra, resident band at the Mansfield Palais.

Staff at the Princess Cinema in Lincoln Road in 1938.

The City Cinema in Bridge Street shortly after it was completed in 1927.

The Arcadian Follies make a colourful picture in 1932. Crowds flocked to their comedy, song and dance shows. The Arcadian Follies was an end-of-the-pier show who performed in Blackpool during the summer months before World War Two. For a number of years they visited Peterborough for a winter season, performing at the Empire Theatre. The Follies cast became well known in the city and put on a Christmas party for needy children.

The Broadway Kinema just after it was completed in 1913.

The luxurious interior of the City Cinema in 1956, but soon it had to be modernised to accommodate the new widescreen.

Staff at the Princess Cinema in October, 1936. The film showing was *Dancing Feet*.

Twice Nightly was the boast, and it must have been hard work for the stars performing at The Hippodrome in the heyday of Music Hall. The bill on this occasion included the legendary Marie Lloyd. The Hippodrome stood on the site of the present day Tesco supermarket.

They couldn't believe their eyes. This audience at The Embassy picked up their special glasses to watch a new fangled 3D film which promised that the action would jump right out of the screen. Most people ended up with headaches and eyestrain and the whole gimmick didn't last long.

Once it was The New England Cinema which closed in 1966, but new owners changed it to the Imperial in 1971 when it specialised in showing Asian films for the local community. This is a 1981 picture of the cinema which is now closed.

Sorry about the crack across the old negative, but this is a rare picture of Broadway and its entertainment palaces in the 1920s.

Peterborough Lido Swimming Pool which opened in 1936 to provide healthy swimming facilities after a campaign lasting many years and to stop people swimming in the river. This is a 1990 picture.

A behind-the-scenes shot at The Embassy Theatre in the 1940s.

Classroom Days

We cant help with these very old pictures, other than to say that they are all pictures of pupils taken at Peterborough schools and they date back to before World War One. We can tell from the plaque held by the children in the last picture in sequence of four however that it was of children at the Boys Central National School, Peterborough and it is dated 1904.

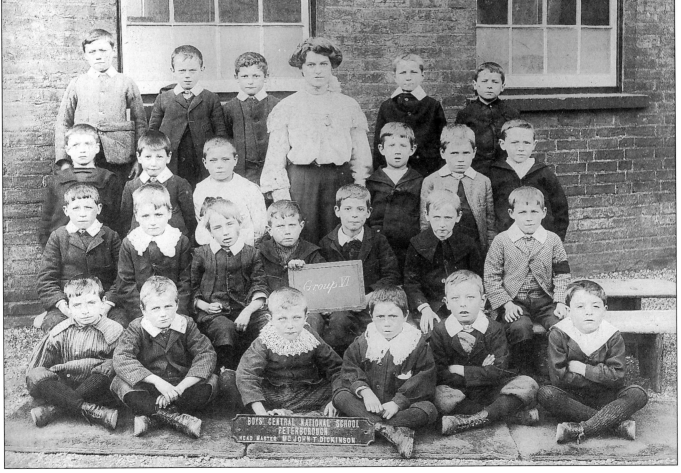

Another busy day in class at West Town School and the pupils broke off from doing their sums (see the blackboard) to pose for this picture.

A Kings School group in 1900.

A group of children at Dogsthorpe School in the 1920s.

Girls learning shorthand at Mrs Bean's Peterborough Commercial School in 1939.

An historic picture of the Peterborough Kings School staff towards the end of the 19th century when mortar boards, gowns and side whiskers gave distinction to the scholastic profession.

Kings School staff pictured in the 1960s. In the front is headmaster Rev Cecil Harrison. He was head for 18 years from 1951 and died in 1986.

Sorry, we cant help with identification on this school group, but we thought it was such a good picture of the little lads – most of them in nice white collars.

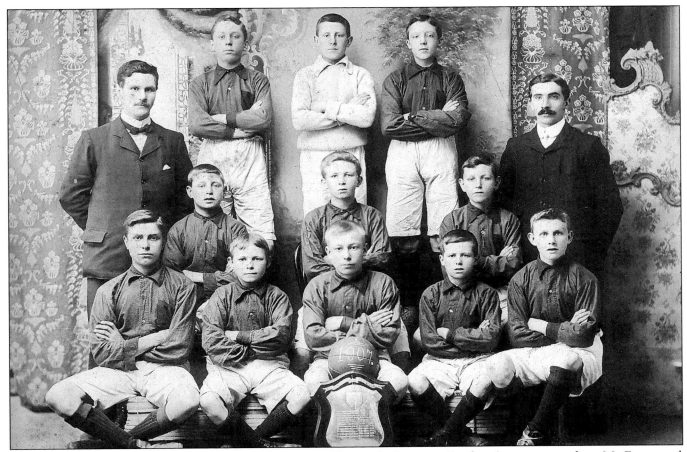

New England Boys School football team proudly show off a trophy in 1907. On the picture are teachers Mr Evans and Mr Whitticase.

Old Fletton School lads pictured in 1952.

Lincoln Road Boys School staff picture.

Class room shot of the County Grammar School for Girls.

Farcet Church of England School, *c.*1945.

St John's School, Stanground, in 1905.

St Mark's School 1936-37.

Hunts County Secondary School, Fletton in 1927.

Woodston School group *c.*1889. The teacher is Mrs Davies.

St Augustine's Church of England School, Wharf Road, Woodston, *c.*1950.

New Fletton School, Oundle Road, Peterborough.

All Saints School group taken in 1912.

An exterior view of the County Grammar School for Girls in 1911 when a game of tennis was in full swing.

Old Fletton School, High Street in 1972.

The old Peterborough Training College in what is now Peterscourt, opposite the current market.

Three heads of the County Grammar School for Girls pictured at a Golden Jubilee event in 1954.

Orton Longueville School opening ceremony in 1961 being addressed by Alderman Wesley Blake in the main hall.

Peterborough British School in Cobden Street in summer 1903.

Royal Visitors

The city seemed to be filled to bursting with people in the streets, there were 6,000 and more in the Market Place alone in 1897, celebrating Queen Victoria's Diamond Jubilee.

A scene in the Market Place showing civic dignitaries preparing for the Diamond Jubilee event.

People board a horse-drawn omnibus in Cromwell Road to take part in the procession into Westgate and the Market Place for the 1897 celebrations.

Flags are waving and some people shelter under umbrellas because of the blazing sun as they mingle in Market Place to join the rest of the country in paying homage to the Queen in 1897.

A group of Stanground residents pictured opposite the Ferry Boat Inn in North Street before going to a party to celebrate the Jubilee.

Ladies in straw boaters pedal past the decorated Vine Restaurant in Church Street to join the celebrations for the Queen of Queens.

To cheers from onlookers the great procession makes its way along Cromwell Road.

Narrow Street was a blaze of colour with bunting and the flags of the Commonwealth fluttering in the warm breeze as everyone hailed Queen Victoria.

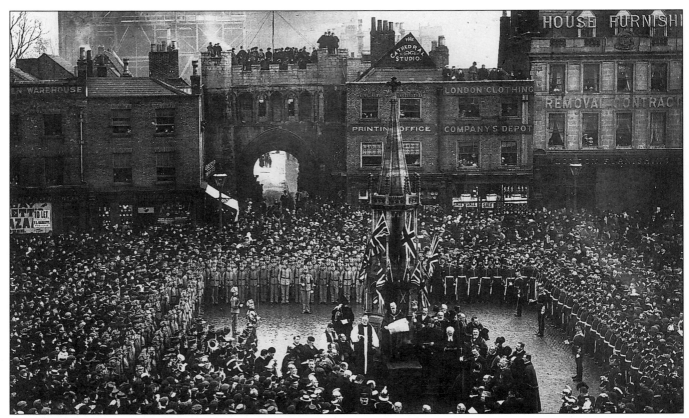

Another day, another era but the city was celebrating again. The occasion was the proclamation of King Edward VII in February 1901. The Market Place (now Cathedral Square) was again the focus of events as the Mayor, Mr G. C. W. Fitzwilliam, stood on the steps of the Gates Memorial to read the official proclamation.

Peterborough Guildhall overshadowing another celebration. Here in the summer of 1911 saw the Mayor, Colin C. E. Crawley, preparing to lead celebrations for the Coronation of King George V.

Coronation decorations in Cowgate, Peterborough, on June 21, 1911.

A mighty traction engine with a banner proclaiming George V pulls a float with a giant crown on top along Broad Bridge Street in 1911.

Long Causeway decked out for the visit of the Prince of Wales, later to be the Duke of Windsor, in July, 1923.

The Prince of Wales inspecting army cadets at Peterborough Showground, on his 1923 visit.

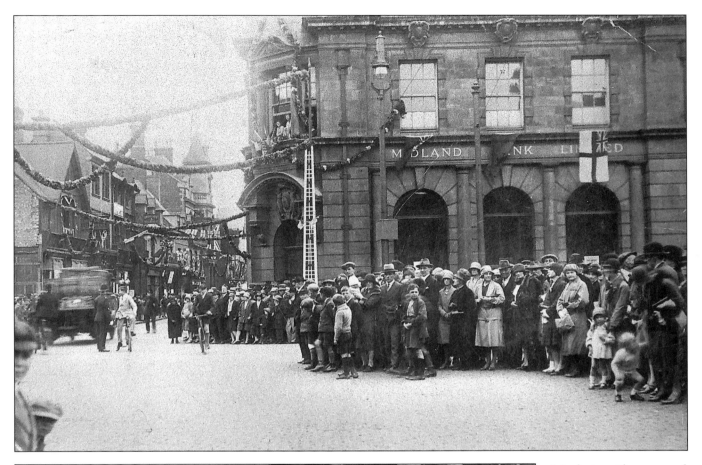

Market Place and Narrow Street was alive with excitement and colour again to mark Civic Week in 1929.

The Duke of Kent (then Prince George) opening an extension to Peterborough power station when he visited the city during Civic Week in June, 1929. On the left is the Marquess of Exeter (Lord Paramount of the Liberty of Peterborough) and on the right are Councillor Arthur Craig (before he was knighted), and Mr Frank Hodges, a member of the old Central Electricity Board.

The Mayor A. H. Mellows raised his hat and the drums rolled for the Proclamation of King George VI in 1936.

It was time for the next generation as the Proclamation of Queen Elizabeth II was read on the steps of the Town Hall by Mayor, G. R. Chamberlain, in 1952.

Peterborough was a sea of colour once more and Bridge Street was festooned with bunting to mark the Coronation of Queen Elizabeth II in 1953.

A fancy dress competition at Maxey House to mark the Coronation. The young girl at the front of the picture is the village's Coronation Queen and she is flanked by her escorts.

The Duke (rear) and Duchess (front right) of Gloucester mingle with the crowds at Barnwell Gymkhana in the 1960s. These most 'local' of Royals lived close by and were very much part of the village scene.

Prince Charles chats to Roy Bird the Secretary of the East of England Agricultural Society on a visit to the East of England Show at Alwalton Showground in 1978.

Prince Philip pictured on a visit to the East of England Show in 1970.

Princess Anne, a keen horsewoman in her own right (Olympic medallist) attends Burghley Horse Trials in 1978.

Princess Anne visiting Burghley Horse Trials again in 1979.

Her Royal Highness, The Princess Royal, unveiling a plaque to mark the opening of the national Deaf Blind and Rubella Association home for sensory handicapped people in Paston in March, 1991. Princess Anne was patron of the association.

These two pictures show children from Dogsthorpe celebrating the 1953 Coronation of Queen Elizabeth II.

Princess Elizabeth with Lord De Ramsey, Show President at the 1951 Peterborough Agricultural Show.

Queen Elizabeth's first visit to Peterborough as a reigning monarch in March 1975. It was also the first the city had received from any reigning monarch. Queen Elizabeth was attending the Maundy Service at the Cathedral.

The Queen did a walkabout in Bridge Street during her 1975 visit receiving flowers from Julie Swift, daughter of Councillor Charles Swift.

The Queen waves to the crowds at the East of England Show at Alwalton in 1991.

Royal visitors to the Peterborough Show of 1932, the Duke of York (later King George VI) and the Duchess.

The Queen Mother visits Peterborough Show and the flower show which she always loved, in 1956.

The Queen Mother, flanked by East of England Agricultural Society officials, visits the East of England Show in 1983.

To the delight of the crowds the Queen Mother toured the Showground in 1983 in an open topped vehicle.

A superb portrait of the Queen Mother at the 1992 East of England Show when she still enjoyed touring the various stands – and the flower show in particular.

Sporting Days

Off to the match, these supporters were all dressed up and off to see Fletton United in the 1920s.

Fletton United – forerunners of Posh – in 1925.

The Posh team of the 1938-39 season.

Peterborough United players line up for a photo shoot in the early 1940s.

A rare action picture from a Peterborough United clash with Northampton away from home in the early 1940s. This is Northampton scoring a goal.

A Posh team picture from the 1950-51 season.

The magical Stanley Matthews treated the crowds to a display of his skill in a benefit match at the Peterborough United ground in 1956.

The Posh team winning Division Four for the first time in 1961.

Terry Bly puts another one in the back of the net for Posh at London Road. Bly scored a record-breaking 52 goals when Posh won the Division Four title in their first season in the Football League in 1960-61.

Here is the greatest team of individuals ever to grace London Road. Over 7,000 Posh fans turned up in April 1970 to watch Ian Crawford's star-studded testimonial side beat Posh 7-4. Pictured with Crawford, from the left, are Bobby Moore, Terry Venables, Johnny Haynes, Maurice Setters, Martin Peters, Geoff Hurst, Derek Dougan, Ron Springett, Rodney Marsh and Frank Rankmore.

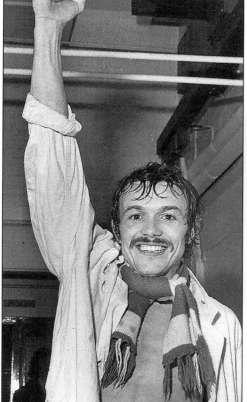

John Cozens punches the air after skippering Posh to the Division Four title in the 1973-74 season.

Bruce Grobbelaar is beaten and Garry Kimble sticks the ball in the back of the net to give Posh a famous 1-0 victory over might Liverpool at London Road in the League Cup in the 1991-92 season.

Posh players celebrate in the dressing room after that memorable League Cup win against the former European champions.

In contrast, Posh battle it out with non-League Kingstonian behind closed doors at London Road in 1992. The FA Cup first round match, which Posh originally won 9-1, had to be replayed after a coin was thrown on to the pitch. Posh won without the fans, 1-0.

We're on our way to Wembley! That's what Posh players and fans were singing here after beating Huddersfield in the Division Two Play-off semi-final in 1991-92.

King Kenny grabs the winner. Kenny Charlery scores the goal that gave Posh that 2-1 Wembley win over Stockport.

Posh's greatest moment – the 1991-92 side celebrate their Wembley win over Stockport County in the Division Two Play-off Final.

Posh celebrated their promotion to Division One by touring the city in an open-topped bus on the day after their Wembley victory.

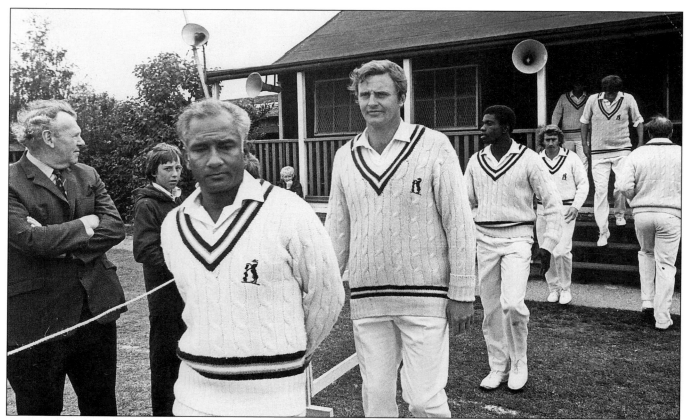

West Indies captain Rohan Kanhai leads his Warwickshire side out at Alma Road in 1974 – the last time Northants played a county match in Peterborough. It was a Sunday League game and Northants won by 40 runs with local lad Alan Tait hitting 102 not out.

Alvin Kallicharan signs autographs for Peterborough cricket fans at the Northants v Warwickshire match at Alma Road.

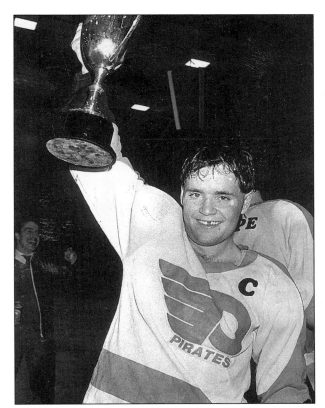

John Lawless, who played one of the leading roles in promoting ice hockey in Peterborough during the 1980s, is pictured with the Heineken League Division One Championship trophy which the Pirates won in 1985.

Richard Greer and John Davies (seated), two members of the Peterborough Panthers team in their first season of speedway in 1970, are pictured in 1972 after being called up by England.

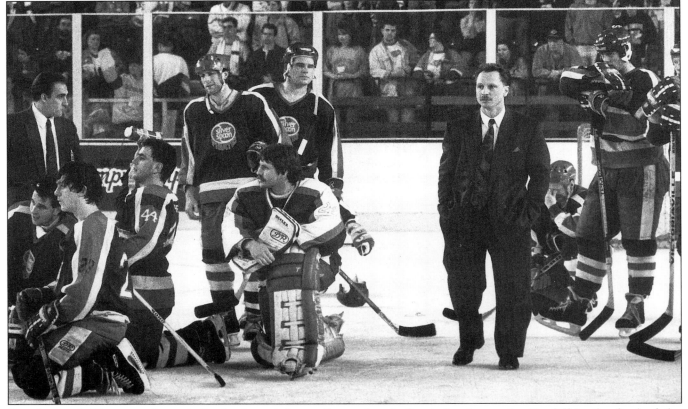

Peterborough Pirates and coach Rocky Saganiuk are disappointed after being beaten by Cardiff in the final of the Wembley Play-offs in April 1981.

Chatteris boxer Dave 'Boy' Green pictured with members of his fan club after winning a British title in 1976. Green twice went on to fight for the world title.

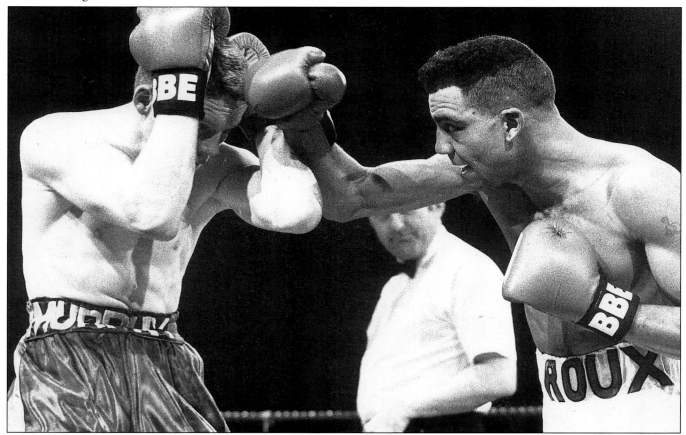

City boxer Gary De Roux hits out during his memorable British title win in London in March 1991. He beat Sean Murphy in five rounds to take the featherweight crown.

Former King's School pupil Paul Barber struck Olympic gold in Seoul in 1988 with the GB men's hockey team. He is pictured here with the bronze he won four years earlier in Los Angeles.

Geoff Capes, the policeman from Holbeach, shows off his Commonwealth Games gold medal to children Lewis and Emma. Geoff won the shot putt at the 1974 Games in Christchurch with a new British record of 68 feet.

Competitors in the inaugural Round The City Road Race line up in March 1951. It was to be the first of many.

Eastern Avenue residents give the Great Eastern Run competitors a helping hand in 1988.

Some of the runners who enjoyed the Great Eastern Run in 1990 set off in Long Causeway.

The start of the 12th Great Eastern Run in 1993.

Giovanni Rizzo, the popular distance runner from Nene Valley Harriers, celebrates after winning a fourth successive Great Eastern Run in 1992. The popular half-marathon race around the streets of Peterborough was the highlight of the city's sporting calendar from 1982 to 1995.

Steve Davis (23) received a tumultuous standing ovation when he turned up at the Posh Club to play Peterborough's Mark Wildman the day after he had just lifted the World Snooker Championship for the first time in 1981. Wildman, a world billiards champion, won the match 5-3.

Peterborough Police Quoits Club and Stamford Town Club at a match in 1890. The winner was PC Grimes.

Quoit team at Eastgate Quoit House Ground with their trophies. Note some of the wide-brimmed cowboy-style hats to keep the sun out of the players' eyes.

The Peterborough Ladies Hockey Club in 1925.

The lads (and some lasses) of Peterborough Cycling Club in 1938.